The Bleeding Heart Diaries

By Sameh Abdallah

ISBN: 978-0-6152-0873-2

Copyright (c) 2008 Sameh Abdallah
Permission is granted to copy, distribute and/or modify this document
under the terms of the GNU Free Documentation License, Version 1.2
or any later version published by the Free Software Foundation;
with no Invariant Sections, no Front-Cover Texts, and no Back-Cover Texts.
A copy of the license is included in the section entitled "GNU
Free Documentation License". If any poetry is redistributed I must be asked for permi
sion first and there shall be no resale of any of the work contained in this book.
For contact information please E-mail me at Abdallahs1@yahoo.com

Author's Thoughts

Poetry is anything you want it to be. Today anyone can put a few words on paper that make a small amount of sense and call it a poem. So what separates one poem from another? It's not only the meaning behind the words or if the words rhyme or not.

When you write poetry you should write it for the only reader that matters, yourself. That is what separates one poet from another. The poet that writes for the public eye and the poet that writes for himself. The poet that writes for the public eye constantly re-writes his work to gain approval from others and is never mindful of why he or she even writes in the first place. The poet that writes for himself or herself alone writes because it is a part of themselves, just as much as their arm or leg is. They write because if they don't it's as if they were suffocating and they do so without any sense or caring of what the public eye thinks of their work.

If you're going to bleed then bleed from your heart"--Sameh Abdallah

ndex

Index

Index

"The Bleeding Heart Diaries"

Page after page
Is written with his heart.
Whether you start at the end
Or end at the start.

His emotions and feelings
Arranged all in lines.
That talk about life
And searching for signs.

He talks about love
That he is still yet to find.
And how all his thoughts
Are trapped in his mind.

His heart is his pen
And his blood is the ink.
And the words that are written
Will cause you to think.

His soul and his heart
And all that was said.
Are in the bleeding heart diaries
Just waiting to be read.

"A Days Dream"

I sit outside your window
Waiting for you to wake.
I'll wait forever patiently
And hope its no mistake.

They say one look into your eyes
Can make a man feel free
And all it takes is just one touch
To make the heart agree.

I know I'm nothing special.
I know I can't compare.
But if the chance is given
I'll show you that I care.

For now I wait outside your window
And dream of you as my bride.
To hope you awake from slumber
And see what waits outside.

"12/7/07"

12/7/07
It's the day that time stood still.
The day I try and forget
But know I never will.

It's when I gave you my heart
And you threw it away.
And what causes me always
To remember that day.

I never saw it coming
As if I were blind.
As you took out your knife
And stabbed from behind.

The day you gave me this hole
That no person could fill.
Yet I'm still alive
Though you went for the kill.

I thought that I loved you.
That you were my way to heaven.
Until I'm forced to remember
12/7/07.

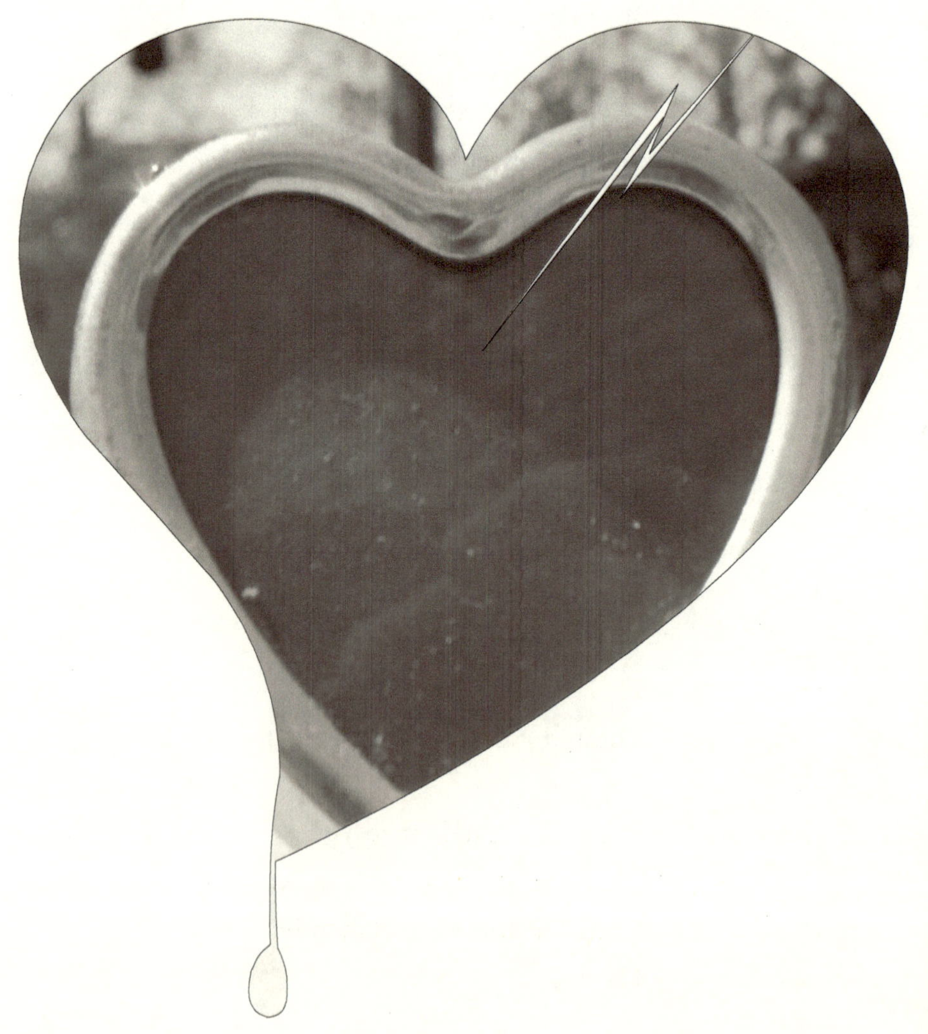

"A Dreamer's Wish"

If only things were different
Then maybe I'd win her heart.
If only things were different
I know we'd never part.

If only the stars were closer
I would put them in her eyes.
For beauties such as these
Do not belong in skies.

If only every flower
Were as beautiful as her face.
I would follow her every foot step
And put them in her place.

And if only all these words
Could match the radiance of her soul.
I would write an endless novel
To make my world feel whole.

But if only things were different
These dreams would all come true.
And I would follow every one
Until they lead me all to you.

"Clocks"

Being alive can kill you.
It's taken years off of my life.
And the moments that can thrill you
Will eventually bring you strife.

Minutes into hours
And hours into days.
Walking around forever
In this unforgiving maze.

The clocks all seem to taunt me
As they count my life away.
Pushing me towards tomorrow
When I'm trying to hold onto today.

If time is of the essence
Then why does it always slip?
Shoving you over the edge
And making you lose your grip.

And when I think all is well
And my heart has just mended.
I soon then discover
That my time left has ended.

"A Place In Her Heart"

Her hair crashes down upon her shoulders
Like the waves that are in the sea
And her eyes light the way to the darkest corners
Like the stars that are flying free.

Her body is like a road that is filled with curves
And is paved with the finest gold.
Her hands are like silk woven from the softest material
And to which they broke the mold.

Her lips are like a sunset
That never faded into night.
And tells me of a story
That no poet could recite.

And her soul is like a maze
To which there is no end.
Like an eternity of days
Without the time to spend.

If only I knew just where to go,
If only there were a chart.
That could lead me to my destiny.
To a place within her heart.

"A Poem To The World"

This is a poem to all who know.
To all who can see past the daily façade.
Who look to the sky
Looking for answers from God.

This is a poem for all who suffer
And don't know why.
To all who feel the pain
Wishing they would die.

This is a poem to all who have loved
And not been loved in return.
To wish for that one person
But to only feel the burn.

This is a poem to the world
That left me to die.
That left me sitting there wondering why.

This is my poem to the world.

"All I Need"

If there is such a place as Heaven
It would be within your eyes.
For all it takes is just one look
And the sorrow in me dies.

Your smile makes the sun shine bright
And brings happiness to my soul.
You take what was my broken heart
And suddenly make it feel whole.

Your skin is just as soft as silk
And no fabric could compare.
And your beauty is so astounding
That it causes crowds to stare.

Your soul is made of flowers
That were planted in the sky.
And your heart is made of gold
That no king could ever buy.

And all together your perfect
That any judge would concede.
For your all that I could ever want
And all I will ever need.

"Beautiful"

She's beautiful in every way
Her eyes just seem to shine.
She's got me down like a dog again
And I beg to call her mine.

She's beautiful and that's no mistake,
It's true that is no lie.
She floats around on angel wings
Upon the heavenly sky.

She's beautiful and anyone can see
It's really not hard to tell.
She's so beautiful and I'm just me,
It's like comparing heaven to hell.

She's beautiful and elegant
Like a princess in my dreams.
And she looks like she's so happy too
But nothing is as it seems.

She's beautiful and it's been said.
Over again it's been stated.
She's beautiful and that's a fact
But beauty's so overrated.

"Lament"

This sorrow inside me
Taking control.
This pain that is evident
Swallowing me whole.

My soul ever fading
My spirit forever gone.
Like an evening with no sunset
Like a morning with no dawn.

Flowers have no color
And music has no sound.
Life no longer has meaning
And hope can not be found.

With you no longer with me
I slowly die each day.
You were my purpose of living
Now the reason for my dismay.

Now all that I have
Is this pain and torment.
Always inside me
I will forever lament.

"Chasing Stars"

Just give me one chance
To show you my worth.
For to get to you
I'd move Heaven and Earth.

Let the mountains crumble
And the oceans disappear.
For nothing else exists
Whenever you are near.

If the clouds caused you sadness
I would wipe them from the sky.
And if you ever started crying
I know that I would die.

And if a sunset lacked in beauty
I would gaze at you instead.
For your look could heal the weak
And give life back to the dead.

But in the end I'm left to wonder
If you could ever heal these scars.
Or if I'll be left here in the darkness
Grasping at the stars.

"Evolution"

It's over now.
My time is done.
I've felt the pain.
You've had your fun.

I've listened to your stories
Heard all your lies.
I'm tired of pretending
I'm breaking our ties.

I really cared for you.
A truth all told too well.
I showed you a part of heaven
You gave me a piece of hell.

I'll live another day.
I'll see another dawn.
I guess it's as they say
You never know what's missing
Until what your missing is gone.

"Pin Cushions"

Were hearts meant for loving?
Or for storing needles instead?
For when it comes to matters of the heart
I think I'd rather be dead.

All hearts just deceive you
They all just push you into love.
But then we all soon discover
That the push becomes a shove.

Then your world just seems so happy
And nothing could bring you down.
Until that smile you are showing
Turns into a frown.

Because the one your heart had fallen for
Had a needle with your name.
And when you least expected it
They quickly took their aim.

And then you're left to wonder
Just why you're so depressed.
When the reason it all started
Was because of the pin cushion in your chest.

"Darkness"

What people are so afraid of
Yet what many others seek.
It could give you all the strength you need
And at the same time make you weak.

What once was my enemy
Had now become my friend.
For the light that had existed
Has finally found it's end.

Like the coming of a sunset
The darkness overtakes the light.
Until all that was visible
Visibly loses sight.

The heart within my body
Once shining with a glow.
Has become so dim with sorrow
That it has nothing left to show.

Now left here in the shadows
Under the cover of the night.
Just a man engulfed in darkness
Searching for the light.

"The Missing Piece"

From the moment life began
He could feel like no other.
The world he knew was shattered.

He would walk the empty roads
And search the deserted sea.
He would climb the highest mountains
Yet never find the key.

He would look to the sky
But only see a cloud.
Walk through the forest
But only see the trees.

All the world was searched
There was nothing more to do.
That one piece was missing
This was all that he knew.

What is this piece?
Oh! Where can it be?

He searched the empty roads.
He searched the deserted sea.
Yet he would never find that missing piece.

For that missing piece is me.

"Wonders Of The World"

I have scaled all the mountains.
I have crossed all the seas.
I have conquered most of my problems
With very little ease.

I have seen the sun set in Europe
And the moon rise in Spain.
I've seen the Aurora Borealis
And the Rain forest's rain.

I have walked on the pyramids of Egypt
And China's great wall.
I've seen most of everything
And thought I had seen it all.

But never in my life
Have I witnessed such beauty.
As my heart stands still
And forgets its eternal duty.

And as I gaze into your eyes
I know that it is true.
That no matter where I go
It all leads back to you.

"Breathe No More"

The cold never ceases
Chilling me to my soul.
Like a puzzle with no pieces
Leaving no way to be whole.

The light now only blinds me.
The darkness now my friend.
Seeking refuge from existence.
Only looking for the end.

What once had been my sunshine
Had now become my rain.
And any feelings left of happiness
Have quickly turned to pain.

The sorrow never ending
Tearing me apart.
And a knife forever digging
Deep within my heart.

I used to be alive
With everything to believe.
Until you took away my air
Leaving nothing left to breathe.

"Dear God"

Dear God,
This is my first letter
And all that I ask of you
Is can you please make things better?

Can you take away my pain
And tell me it's alright?
Can you take away the darkness
When there is very little light?

Could you heal all my wounds
Even though I'm not bleeding?
Give me all that I ask
And all I am needing?

Dear God it's been weeks
And I still feel the pain.
I can't see the sunshine.
It's still pouring rain.

I still look for answers
As I sit here and wait.
But dear God it's been forever
And I fear it's too late.

"Hopeless Romantic"

Why do they call us hopeless romantics
When there's nothing romantic about us at all.
For it seems that we are just hopeless
When we set our selves up for the fall.

We pour our hearts into a girl
As if she were the queen.
And all we get back in return
Is that all too familiar routine.

And it hurts so much to be left in the dust
That we swear it wont happen again.
But our hopes inside say we'll be fine
Yet it seems we'll never know when.

Maybe one day I'll find a girl
That likes me for being the same.
Just a hopeless romantic guy that dreams
Of the losing the hopeless part of his name.

"Save The World"

Why do the people suffer
And tears of pain fill their eyes?
When instead of beautiful clouds
Only missiles fill the skies.

Why are there children
That run scared every night.
Not trying to avoid a monster
But trying to avoid a fight.

When will they understand
When we bleed it's all the same.
That you don't have to find happiness
By causing others pain.

When did our dreams become a nightmare
And our nightmares not a dream.
And all the so called truths
Are not quite what they seem.

People keep on dying
As grown men play with toys.
That block out children's laughter
With unforgiving noise.

Yet all the people suffer
Engulfed in all the fear.
Waiting forever patiently
For a hero to appear.

"Not Enough"

I'm not feeling much
Except for this pain.
It's like I'm on the right track
But on the wrong train.

See I don't have much to offer
There's really not much to give
But whenever I look into her eyes
I know without her I can not live.

But I am merely a peasant
And she deserves a king.
For I'm like an ocean with no water
And like a bird without a wing.

She deserves jewelry
That shines as bright as her gorgeous eyes
And a kingdom filled with servants
That floats upon the heavenly skies.

But I am simply a dreamer
And my journey is too rough.
I only wished I was the one she loved
But it seems I am not enough.

القرآن الكريم

"My Autobiography"

He's a vision to some
Yet a lover to none.
And all the pain in his eyes
Echoes miles through the skies.

Doesn't know where it starts
For he walks without charts.
And he travels alone
Treading through the unknown.

On his heart there's a scar
That can be seen from afar.
Yet it beats so alive
Only wanting to strive.

It's like a story never told
Never having a chance to get old.
And the words that are there
Just get lost in the air.

Yet he lives with a smile
But only for a while.
For every soul must transcend
And every story has it's end.

"Slowly Dying"

Why does it feel
Like the world is ending.
As if all the scars I've endured
Are not even worth mending.

It's as if my life means nothing
As if I never had a soul.
As if everything is spinning,
Completely out of control.

Now the days seem darker
And the nights are too cold.
As my life gets heavier
And harder to hold.

For the ropes that have held me
Are starting to unwind
And all my reasons for living
Are getting harder to find.

For every second I am without you
Makes me want to cry.
And the soul that lives inside me
Starts to slowly die.

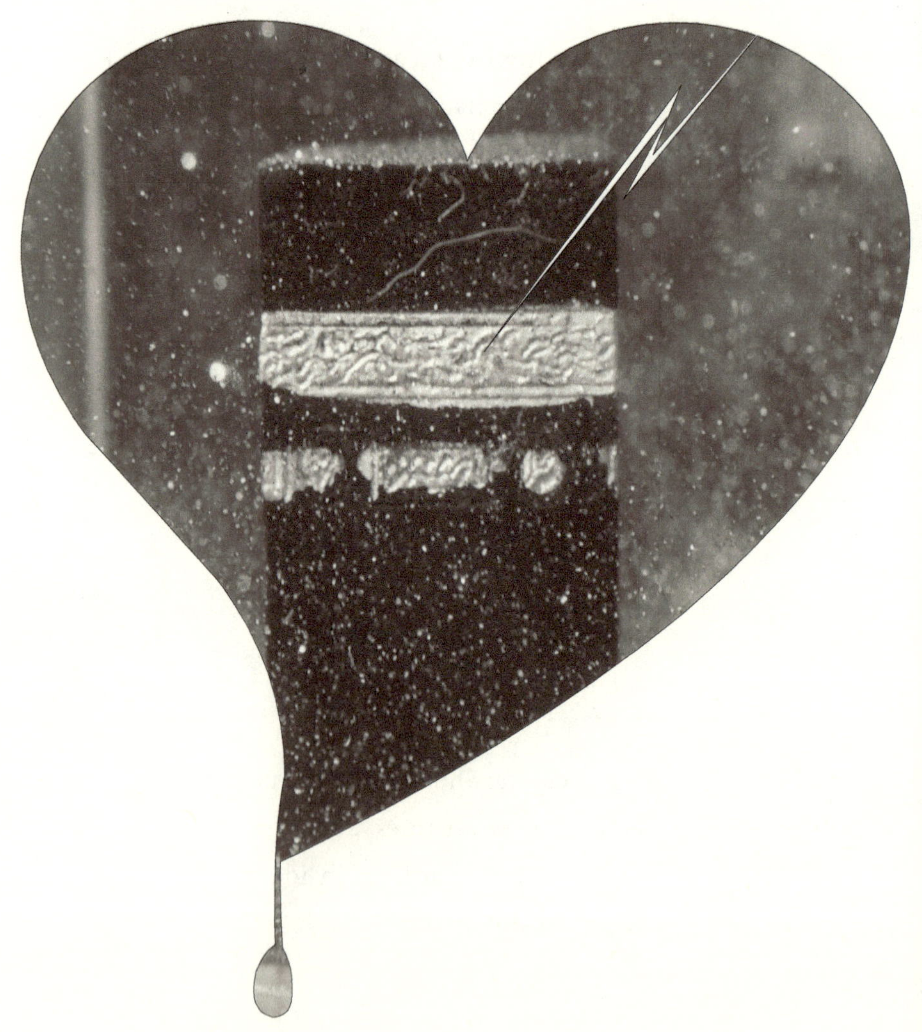

"Dear God: The Second Letter"

Dear God
This is letter number two.
I sent to you the first one
But I doubt it got to you.

I've endured all the pain
And walked through the fire.
Yet I still feel the same
And lack what I desire.

You gave me a woman
And then took her away.
You set me on the path
And then led me astray.

Whenever I am happy
It quickly disappears.
And whenever I search for answers
I can't see through the tears.

Dear God I've been patient
And I hope that you agree.
Because it's hard to keep on breathing
When you're drowning in the sea.

"One Wish"

Imagine having one wish
To finally get what you've always wanted.
To be able to make your dreams come true
And not care if you go and flaunt it.

Many might wish for treasure
For everyone always loves gold.
But I wouldn't waste my wish like that
Because that wish could easily be sold.

Others might wish for greatness
To have the power to rule it all
But those people are never really happy
Because everything to them is too small.

Some would wish for the power to fly
To soar on the skies above.
But they don't know that the real way to fly
Is in finding your one true love.

Now you might be wondering
If I had that wish what I would do?
I would get on my knees and look to the sky
And just wish for only you.

"She Doesn't Know"

She doesn't know
Why I never sleep
Because I've fallen into her eyes
And I have gotten too deep.

She doesn't know
That when I pray every night
I only ask for God
To make sure she's alright.

She doesn't know
About all the pain that I hide.
For I don't show my feelings
So that I don't get denied.

She doesn't know
That I would give everything in my life
To make sure she is happy
And to take away her strife.

She doesn't know
That my heart has stood still.
Because she doesn't know I love her
And I doubt she ever will.

"Crashing Down"

If the stars stopped shining
Down upon your face
I would light up every one of them
And put them in their place.

If the roads grow narrow
And harder to walk.
I would take you to the sky
To fly like a hawk.

If you ever get scared
Of the shadows of the night
I'll be right there to protect you
And make sure you're alright.

If you ever get lonely
And filled with despair
Just call out my name
And I will be there.

If the world all around you
Starts to crash all around
Just look in your heart
And I will be found.

"No More Heroes"

This world is full of sadness
For I could feel it's pain.
It wears a mask of happiness
As it's people go insane.

They no longer smile
Because they've forgotten how.
And they can't ask any questions
That the others wont allow.

When evil and corruption
Are embedded in their hearts.
And everyone feels lost
Even with the greatest charts.

Where are all the heroes
To save us from the pain?
That bring about the sunshine
And take away the rain.

This world could use a hero
To rise and lend a hand
And when there's no more room for heroes
I will take stand.

"Sunshine"

As if God had gathered all his angels
And sent the best one of all to me.
As if there was a lock around my heart
And you were the only key.

Now the world is so much brighter
And everything is clear.
And my heart can't stop from smiling
Whenever you are near.

Now I'm flying without wings
And soaring through the sky.
Feeling like the king of all the kings
Even though I'm a simple guy.

The birds are always singing
And the flowers smell so sweet.
And you've become the cooling shade
In the unforgiving heat.

You're what takes away the darkness
And what causes words to rhyme.
And whenever I am with you
The sun will always shine.

"Truly, those who have faith
and do righteous deeds
will the Most Gracious endow
with Love"
rat Maryam (1

"Eternity"

If only the world would just stop turning
To give me eternity in your eyes.
For I would pay a price twice yearning
To be forever without good-byes.

If only my heart would beat once more
To let me know I'm alive.
To feel a feeling lost so long
To make me want to thrive.

If only I couldn't wake from this dream
To a life without you there.
Then I would shed a thousand tears
To show how much I care.

If only forever were just a little longer
I'd spend it with you there.
But the eyes of eternity eternally slumber
And leave me with despair.

"No One Knows But Me"

I lay awake.
Still not yet asleep.
Thinking of what is to be.

These thoughts consume
And could fill up the sea.
Yet nobody knows this but me.

I see what's to come
But it changes so fast.
So this world is no guarantee.

If I could go back
I wouldn't think twice.
Yet nobody knows this but me.

But all that I want
Is to be with you there.
I pray that you will soon see.

And that is why I lay here at night.

Yet nobody knows this but me.

"Just Perfect"

If I could perfectly capture
The stars in her eyes
I would perfectly place them
In the heavenly skies.

And they would perfectly light up
The way to her heart.
The most perfect example
Of a perfect work of art.

I would gaze at her perfection
For hours at a time.
And wonder forever
Just when she'd be mine.

I would think of the words
That would be perfect to say.
And how I'd perfectly put on
A perfect display.

Yet I began to realize
She would never hear my plea.
For she deserves perfection
That can't be found in me.

"I Belong"

I belong in this moment
Where nobody could ever reach.
I belong in this lesson
That no scholar could ever teach.

I belong in this world
Where magic knows no end
And where the beauty in our hearts
All begin to blend.

I belong in her eyes.
The entrance to heaven's soul,
It is the pinnacle of perfection
And the highest of all goals.

My arms belong around her
Soothing her to sleep
And my heart is longing for her.
Forever for her to keep.

Yet I belong to no one.
A broken man indeed.
Until the moment I am with her
My heart shall always bleed.

"Only Me"

She looks like an angel
And even God would agree.
But heaven is unattainable
For anyone that's like me.

Her eyes shine like stars
That are flying oh so free.
But they don't shine for everyone
Especially not for me.

Her soul is like an ocean
And her heart could fill the sea.
That boats could always sail on
Unless it's sailed by me.

Her beauty is so astounding
That any court room would decree.
She's what dreams were always made of
And could never dream of me.

She's everything I've ever wanted
And this I guarantee.
But I doubt she'll ever know this
Because it's only me.

"Dreaming Out Loud"

Your eyes are so amazing
That they rival the setting sun.
As if beauty spurred from your existence
When the world had just begun.

Your smile can melt the coldest heart
And make a strong man weak.
Your what every man has searched for
And what I will always seek.

I would walk a million miles
Just to see your smiling face.
In hopes that I would one day
Get to hold you in my embrace.

I would give my place in heaven
If it meant eternity with you here.
And I would give a whole king's ransom
So that you never shed a tear.

But I must be only dreaming
For I'm running out of time.
When I awake to this reality
And can no longer call you mine.

"Let It Be"

Let the rain pour down
And wash my sins away.
Let the silence resound
So that God may hear me pray.

Let the sky turn red
Like the color of blood.
Let the oceans come
And bring about a flood.

Let the flowers wilt
And the mountains crumble.
Let a weak man be strong
And a strong man be humble.

Let night become day
And day become night.
Let the lost find their way
And let the blind have their sight.

Let the streams disappear
And the rivers run dry.
Make a world without fear
And then let me die.

"It's All About You"

At night when I dream
I see colors in a beautiful hue
And it tells me of a story
That's all about you.

All the reasons I try
And all the things that I do.
For with every thing that ever mattered
It was all about you.

Any time I ever faltered
I know that I knew,
That I had to go on
To just get to you.

I never believed in heaven.
I didn't think it was true.
But then I always see an angel
Whenever I look at you.

The only reason I write
Is to get my message through.
In hope that you will realize
That this is all about you.

"Blind Sight"

In the shadows of the night
Where the light fears to go
There lives a life to dark to see
Yet seeing is what it knows.

Keen with it's senses
Aware of what's around.
Yet lonely is what its feeling
Because it's never found.

It walks around forever
With hope that someone will see.
And finds the soul that lies within
And tries to set it free.

Yet in a world that's filled with darkness
There eyes just wont adjust.
And the blindness that is given
Is filled with there distrust.

For now it waits forever
In the shadows where it lies
To see if their eyes will open
And see past the disguise.

"Our Final Breath"

I used to think I knew it all
That I was the one on top.
And now my world is spinning
When all I want it to do is stop.

The light now burns my eyes
And the darkness is too dim.
I try to stop from sinking
But I find that I can't swim.

I had a firm hold on this life
Until it slowly slipped away.
I was always on the move
But now all I want is to just stay.

Why were we given eyes
If we insist on being blind?
Thinking that we've seen it all
When there are endless things to find.

If only we all realized
That there's nothing closer to life than death.
Then maybe we will wake up
Before we take our final breath.

"My Heart Is A Pathological Liar"

As if this life wasn't hard enough
Now I have to deal with you.
Will someone please just tell me
What is it that I have to do?

Because my heart just keeps on lying
Directly to my face.
And keeps me running around in circles
Until I lose this race.

It just puts on a convincing smile
And tells me to fall in love.
And will continue to keep on pushing
Until I learn how to shove.

And like a gullible little child
I believe every single word.
And no matter what I tell it
It's as if it never heard.

Yes my heart's just out to get me
Because all it does is lie
And the only time it will ever stop
Is the day I decide to die.

"Escape Reality"

Somewhere life is good
And people always smile
Where the smiles they are wearing
Never goes out of style.

Yet back in this reality
That world is just a dream.
Where instead of joyous laughter
All you hear is a silent scream.

Someone please tell me
Exactly what to do.
To awaken from this nightmare
To a place where skies are blue.

When all the world keeps begging
Yet they don't speak a word
How can we hear their voices
If their voices can't be heard?

So just give me one more glimpse
Of that place where people smile.
So that I can escape from this reality
For just a little while.

"Let Me Bleed"

These memories not forgotten
Embedded in my heart
And every breath that I am taking
Tares me all apart.

This burden I am bearing
Is meant for me alone.
For this sorrow that is in me
Is all I've ever known.

I'm like a flower that has wilted
Without the chance to grow.
Or like a sunset in the evening
With no colors left to show.

The answers that I seek
Are always too far away.
And whenever I reach for happiness
I am left with only dismay.

So left here in these shadows
Just a broken man in need.
With scars around my heart
That remind me just to bleed.

"Purgatory"

I am neither here
Nor am I there.
I am not happy
Yet I do not despair.

I feel nothing
But nothing feels so good.
For whenever I feel
I feel misunderstood.

I am not an outcast
But I just don't belong.
I tried to fit in
I tried for so long.

All that I want
Is to hear a guiding song
Leading me to a place
To find where I belong.

I wait for that day to come
And listen with all my might.
To hope one day I hear that song
And make it all feel right.

"Stand Alone Complex"

Here I stand
Where I have always stood.
With an ambition so fierce
And a will to do good.

Yet it seems I have been standing
Forever all alone.
That the world all around me
Has become the unknown.

I've tried all my life
Just to always do my best.
To always live in shadows
And to never be like the rest.

But it seems that the shadows
Have grown lonely and cold.
And now that ambition that was shining
Leaves nothing to behold.

Now I want more than anything
To find where I belong.
For I will search for all eternity
Until I hear that guiding song.

But it seems that I am dreaming
For my fate is set in stone.
So always in the shadows
I will forever stand alone.

"My Dreams Die Here"

I used to see heaven in your eyes
Now only the hells below.
I used to see so much in you
But now there's nothing left to show.

What happened to the dreams I had
With you standing as my wife?
Now only left with broken memories
And a God forsaken life.

If only things were different
And I could really turn back time
I'd find a way to make things right
A way to keep you mine.

But I'm still only dreaming
And dreams just never last.
For when I try to move on forward
They keep me coming to the past.

Yet I can not forget you
And I don't know what to do.
So I'll just turn my back and walk away
And let my dreams die here with you.

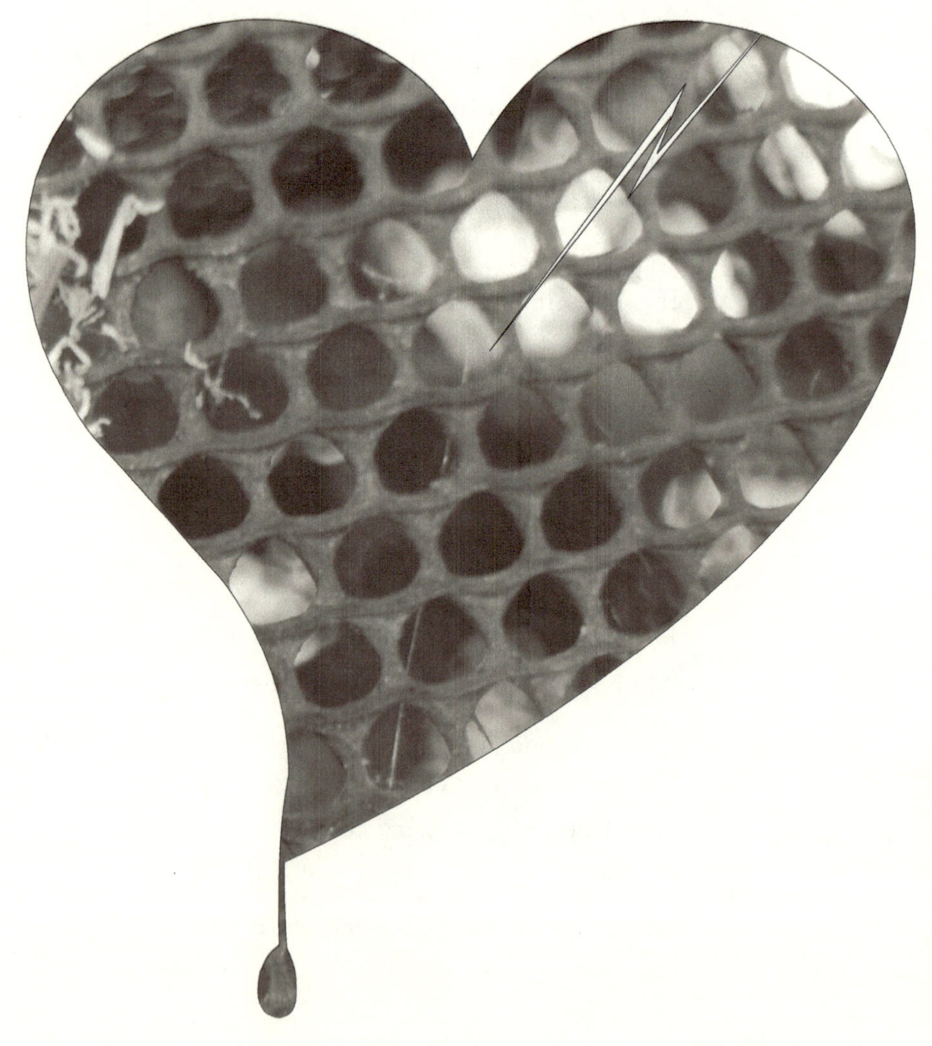

"Eternal Darkness"

The sun has stopped shining.
Only the darkness exists.
And the pain that has ended
Now continues to persist.

The smiles have faded
And the laughter is done.
For the battle I am fighting
Can never be won.

With the darkness around me
The shadows have become my friend.
For the light that was eternal
Had finally found it's end.

Now I can't find my way
Without a light to guide me.
And I can't find any hope
When there is none left inside me.

Now on my damaged heart
Their lies another mark.
As I try to make my way
Through this eternal dark.

"Once Upon a Time"

In your eyes I saw a scene
That was not meant for mortal men.
For only angels could produce such beauty
That could bring such heavenly Zen.

In your soul is where hope resides
And where the kindest of hearts do lay.
For it moves whomever it touches
And removes all of their dismay.

And In your hand you held my heart
That I so readily gave to you.
And took it within your relentless grip
And ripped it into two.

And in my chest is where nothing lays
Just a vacancy that can't be filled.
For when you did that unforgivable act
It's as if I had been killed.

And I used to think you were the one
That there were no mountains left to climb.
And I used to believe all that I had said in the start
But that was just once upon a time.

"Just Pray"

As the sun sets on our hearts
And the shadows all take form.
The dark clouds of existence
Bring about a storm.

The world turned it's back
And then so did we.
Why show us any hope
That no one else can see?

How many more must suffer?
How many lives must we take?
How many tears must come flowing?
How many hearts must we break?

Why can't we all just realize
That we're living just to die?
How will anything ever happen
If no one will even try?

That's why I just sit here
For each and every day
And beg God for an answer
On these shattered knees I pray.

"The Lost Angel"

If heaven had lost an angel
I'd know just where she'd be.
For no other beauty can move mountains
And separate the sea.

She sits around the forests
When the weather is just right
And provides illumination
Through the darkness of the night.

She floats around on angel wings
For her feet never touch the ground.
And when she speaks all the angels sing
From the heavens all around.

Yet even with all her majesty
Tears flow from her eyes.
Like the pain of a hundred sorrows
And the scream of a thousand cries.

Yes if heaven had lost an angel
I'd know just where to turn.
For she is all I have ever wanted
And all I will ever yearn.

"Cigarettes"

Life is like a Cigarette
Because you slowly die each day.
And everyone always tries to quit
But then ends up wanting to stay.

Life is like a cigarette
Because it will continue to just lie.
Making you believe that you're something special
Until you just suddenly die.

Life is like a cigarette
Because you find it harder to breathe each day.
And no matter how hard you try to change
The pain won't go away.

Life is like a cigarette
Because it doesn't care about who you are.
It will kill you without any warning
Or just leave you with a scar.

Life is like a cigarette
Because you suck up all that it can give.
And when you're fighting not to die
It makes too hard for you to live.

"The World Is Not Enough"

I thought you were the one.
My true destiny.
Until you took away the sun
Leaving nothing left to see.

Whenever I was with you
The sun would always shine.
And I would be dreaming of the day
That I would call you mine.

But now I see so clearly
That the day will never come.
And that love is just a gift
That is only meant for some.

And I am not that special
To get that kind of gift.
So now deep inside my heart
Lies an unforgiving rift.

Yet for you I would have climbed mountains
No matter how rough.
I promised you the world
But the world was not enough.

"Eternity's Eyes"

There are moments in this life
Where you wish you could live forever.
When you wish you had eternal bonds
That no thing in this life could sever.

And as I gaze into her eyes
I see more than words can say.
When you find it's too difficult to communicate
Only the truest of hearts can convey.

Oh how I wish to live forever
In that paradise they call your eyes.
And I will try for all eternity
Until all the hope within me dies.

Because no life is worth living
Without you in my heart.
For I would give all that's worth giving
To know that we would never part.

But I fear that I will be left here
To reach my own demise.
When all that I ever wanted
Was to live in eternity's eyes.

"The Girl With Deep Brown Eyes"

She looks to me like heaven
Or the most beautiful sunrise.
She makes me wait forever.
This girl with deep brown eyes.

I only wish to hold her
To never say any good-byes.
For I can't be without her.
This girl with deep brown eyes.

And if ever she was sad
I would hear her distant cries
And would constantly come running
To this girl with deep brown eyes.

If this world was not meant for her
I would take her to the skies
To be among the angels
This girl with deep brown eyes.

Yet I wonder if she'll leave me
To reach my own demise.
When all I ever wanted
Was the girl with deep brown eyes.

"In Your Eyes"

In your eyes
I see the sun.
It's light forever shining
It's beauty second to none.

In your eyes
I see hope like I've never known.
As if the world had never seen sadness
As if its pain had never shown.

In your eyes
I see your soul.
It moves my every being
And swallows me whole.

In your eyes
I am forever lost.
Wishing to forever stay that way
No matter what the cost.

In your eyes
I see my fate.
For I will wait for you forever
And in your eyes is where I will wait.

"Forgotten"

In this life where you can't go back.
Make things right.
Or get back on track.

You mean the best
But do the worst.
Trying so hard.
Ready to burst.

In truth that's told
It's told too true.
Once it's done
You can't undo.

I'll say this forever
And forever it will stay.
It's easier to run
And just go away.

So live your life
And don't you fret.
For when it's forgotten
You don't have to forget.

"I Only Know Her Name"

For the longest time now
My heart had turned to stone.
And I had become so very used to
The feeling of being alone.

The days were all the same
And the nights were always cold.
The Feelings only grew stronger
Without a hand to hold.

I became forever distant.
The shadows my only friend.
As the pain grew more persistent
I prayed to see an end.

Yet at my weakest moment
It's as if God had heard my plea
And sent to me an angel
That only I could see.

She looked at me with her angelic eyes
And took away my pain.
She melted away my frozen heart
In a way I can't explain.

As if I were only dreaming
She vanished as fast as she came.
She took away my sorrow
And only left me her name.

"The Trail of Tears"

I walk this path
To reach her soul.
I tread this trail
To become whole.

I try so hard
To reach her eyes.
To gaze again
At heavenly skies.

Yet the wind of despair
Just blows in my face
And pushes me down
To lessen my pace.

And as I reach my destination
She begins to fade away.
Taking all my happiness
And leaving me dismay.

I then turn to look
To see if she appears
But all that I could see
Are just my trail of tears.

"Handle With Care"

When your heart's made out of glass
People could see right through you.
And when you're trying to hide your secrets
They all just get a clear view.

And no matter how fragile my heart is
It always gets tossed around.
Sometimes I just wish I could take it
And bury it deep in the ground.

But as if my heart were a basketball
I throw it back into the game.
Yet all the people that I throw it to
Toss it right back from where it all came.

And yet I continue to keep on giving
Until there's nothing left of my heart to take.
Which makes me wonder if God had made me
With a heart that was meant to break.

One day I'll write God a letter
That says that all hearts should come with a spare.
Or even at the very least
A note that says "Handle with care."

"I Used To Call Her Sunshine"

I used to call her sunshine
Because she always brightened my day
And would always be my color
Whenever skies were gray.

I used to call her sunshine
Because her smile made me warm
And she would always be my guiding light
Whenever clouds would form.

I used to call her sunshine
Because she took away the rain.
She brought along her happiness
And took away my pain.

I used to call her sunshine
But now I only call her by name
Because I have fall for her beauty
Though I know she's not feeling the same.

I used to call her sunshine
But I seem to always forget.
Whenever a golden sun rises
It will always eventually set.

"I'll Be There"

When the world turns dark
And you don't know what to do.
Just blow a wish into the wind
And I'll be there for you.

When your tears form an ocean
That could fill the whole night's sky.
Just ask a question in your heart
And I'll be there to reply.

When sadness seems so familiar
And happiness seems far away.
Just say a prayer into the sky
And I'll be there to stay.

When you can't go on
And it's too hard to stand.
Just reach out your arm
And I'll hold your hand.

When your road grows narrow
And filled with despair.
Just call out my name
And I will be there.

"Notice Me"

Have you ever noticed a sunset
And the way it takes hold of your heart?
With its beauty just so amazing
That it hurts to know that you'll part.

Have you ever noticed the stars
And how they shine so bright in the sky?
As if they were holding back all the darkness
So that the birds would know where to fly.

Have you ever noticed a summer breeze
And the way it just sooths your soul?
It's like that most important puzzle piece
That you've found to make you whole.

Have you ever noticed the little things
That nobody seems to know?
It's as if everyone just stopped caring
To see what the world has to show.

Yet even if you've noticed it all
There is still one thing you did not see.
For I guess it's not worth noticing to you
Because you're not noticing me.

NO
TRESPASSING
BC Ord. 89-30

"The Love Poet Writes"

Alone in the darkness
With a candle by his side.
He hopes to revive
In his chest what has died.

He whispers his secrets
Into a piece of torn paper.
Grasping at thoughts
That disappear just like vapor.

And with a flick of his wrist
He turns words into melodies.
Simple dreams into deep thoughts
And confusion into sanity.

With the holes in his heart
The words bleed right out.
On that piece of torn paper
He can't do without.

So sitting alone
Under the flickering lights.
With his heart in his hand
The love poet writes.

"The Holocaust of Hearts"

Falling in love must be evil
Because it all just makes you so weak.
Making it harder for you to concentrate
And even harder for you to speak.

You see love is like a game
That it seems I can never win.
That's why I should stop
Before I begin.

But the pain has overcome me
For I have fallen for her hard.
And to continue on this journey
Would leave me only scarred.

So love is just a nightmare
In the form of a distant dream.
And making you think that you could fall in love
Is the underlining theme.

But your hearts just out to get you
And will continue to persist.
Until the day you begin to realize
That true love does not exist.

"Deep Within My Heart"

It's as if time never existed
When I look into your eyes.
As if the sands of time resisted
From falling from the skies.

It's as if the world just has no meaning
Like it does when I'm with you.
As if I thought I had known everything
But really had no clue.

It's as if our hearts beat as one
But God ripped it in two.
And gave one piece to me
And gave the other half to you.

It's as if your beauty gives the sunrise
All of its majestic light
To take away the darkness
That comes during the night.

It's as if I wasn't dreaming
And we wouldn't have to part
But I know I will always keep you
Deep within my heart.

"When Beauty Meets The Beast"

If life were only like a fairy-tale
And I was the handsome king.
Where castles flew upon the clouds
And birds would always sing.

Even if I were that hopeless boy
Who lived among the streets.
That falls in love with a princess
That he thinks he'll never meet.

I would give it all to be that guy
That wins the maiden's heart.
Where no matter what the obstacle
You know they'll never part.

But I am just a mortal man
And she is a radiant queen.
And this is not a fairy-tale
That everyone has always seen.

For I'm afraid to show my love
To put it in the least.
In the fear of what could happen
When the beauty meets the beast.

"My Heart's Plea"

Even in my youngest years
I have felt the pain.
I have shed those tears.

But even in my darkest times
I have always come through.
Pushed you through the fire
Telling you what to do.

Now you no longer listen.
This pain I can no longer relieve.
This road to long to walk.
I cry, I greave.

I beg of you
Don't let me die.
I long to be loved.
I long to fly.

I try so hard
But its so hard to try.
Don't leave me now.
Don't say good-bye.

"Tears Of My Soul"

As if the sun was shining
Yet it gave off little light.
And the days that we were used to
Had faded into night.

When the wreckage in your chest
Leaves little to repair.
And the joys found in life
Now give you nothing but despair.

As if the flowers in a garden
Have no beauty to behold.
And the warm touch of a loved one
Can feel like bitter cold.

When feeling your existence
Never mattered to the rest.
As if God had only cursed you
And left the others blessed.

As if your heart had been removed
Leaving nothing but a hole.
And the tears that you are crying
Are coming from your soul.

"In The Eyes Of An Angel"

If my heart would just start beating
I'd know I were alive.
For its stood so still forever
That it's forgotten how to thrive.

And yet as I gaze into your eyes
My heart begins to flutter.
And all these words I have to say
Become so hard to mutter.

Heaven was only a distant dream
Until I looked into your eyes.
For you must have been an angel
That has fallen from the skies.

I wish I knew the words to say
That could win an angels heart.
For your more beautiful than any flower
And the truest work of art.

But can the eyes of an angel
See the likes of me?
For I am merely human
And that's all that I can be.

"Waterfalls"

Why does it feel
Like I can no longer breathe.
It's as if the soul from inside of me
Is beckoning to leave.

Why can't I seem
To find the words to say.
To tell you how I feel inside
For I try from day to day.

Why can't I find
A way to capture your heart.
To find a way to show to you
That without you I fall apart.

Why can't I be
Everything that you need.
I'll never stop until the day I die
I must not quit until I succeed.

Why must I live
If I am already dead.
For without you there is no hope in sight
Not even a single shred.

But then why do these tears
Come flowing from my eyes
Like waterfalls from heaven
Falling through the skies.

"Ordinary World"

Waking up each morning
Seems harder than before.
When did living life
Become just another chore.

I turned on the TV
And listened to the radio.
Finding everybody rushing
With no where to even go.

What has happened to me.
I'm crazy people say.
It's like I'm the only one in color
Staring at shades of gray.

But I won't cry for yesterday
The tears will only fade away.
Like the stories of the past
All our dreams just don't last.

And in this ordinary world
Where all the people seem alive.
I must turn the other cheek
And just learn how to survive.

"My Despair"

I look for what cannot be found.
I hurt yet I have no wound.
I ask, but receive no answer.

Is life meant to be
All that I cannot see?

When all the world is dark.
When it all just seems too much.
Will their be a hand to hold?
Or will I live my life forever cold?

All these answers I seek.
Oh how I want to find.
But alone I will always live
Forever in my mind.

"You Stole My Heart"

You took my heart
And walked away.
You took it all
And left dismay.

A shell of a man
Is all that is left
With a hole in his chest
As proof of your theft.

Tattered and torn
And ripped all to shreds.
You've tightened your hold
But loosened the threads.

Now I can't keep together
I'm falling to pieces.
Hoping one day
That all of this ceases.

And all I can remember
Is the day we did part.
When you walked away.
And just stole my heart.

"The Man Behind The Words"

I breathe in
Just to let it out.
I whisper words inside me
When I really want to shout.

I have chains that bind me
And hold me to the wall.
Yet if I try and break them
Who will catch me when I fall?

I feel forever lonely
Yet I know I'm never alone.
I try so hard to break free
And show what I've never shown.

I'm a man of many words
With nothing left to say.
And when I reach for happiness
I only grab dismay.

The thoughts that flow inside me
Are like uncontrollable herds.
And to escape from this reality
I hide behind my words.

"The Fine Line"

There is a feeling that everyone gets.
A feeling deep inside.
An emotion that can't be kept.
A secret you can not hide.

It's when your world just makes no sense
And you want to disappear.
When living the life you've lived
Keeps it all from being clear.

For every choice that one must make.
For every decision you must decide.
For every breath that one must take.
For every Jekyll there is a Hyde.

"In My Mind"

In my mind
I can rule it all.
Making peace exist with everyone
So that no one else could fall.

In my mind
I am a hero flying high.
Risking my life for the people
So they wouldn't have to die.

In my mind
I have to do good.
To find a way to change the world
Because I know I should.

In my mind
I am so alone.
Being forever distant
To hide what I've never shown.

In my mind
Is where I am free.
I will be waiting for my destiny
And in my mind is where I'll be.

"Broken Wings"

I can't describe this pain I feel
This sorrow you can't compare.
For what you see in front of you
Is the meaning of despair.

I walk this world from day to day
Not knowing where to go.
For it seems I have lost my destiny
And have nothing left to show.

For she stole my heart without a word
And left me in the dark.
And put me on this lonely road
With this journey to embark.

I try so hard to get to her
But it seems I am without avail.
For it seems that she has disappeared
And left without a trail.

It's as if we were both angels
But my wings just could not soar.
So she left and went to heaven
Gone forever more.

So now I can not reach you
For you are flying in the sky.
Making me wonder if I'll ever see you
For on broken wings I can not fly.

"Lost In The Darkness"

Lost in the darkness
When once I had sight.
Once there was morning
But now endless night.

With no sun left to guide me
I slowly begin to fade.
As I walk through the unknown
In this never ending shade.

It wasn't always like this
For their used to just be light.
Until the moment that you left me
And gave me eternal night.

Now lost here in this darkness
The sorrow grabs hold of my soul.
And drives away my sanity
Until I lose control.

Now I lay here in the void
Until my timely death.
As I whisper that I loved you
With my one and only breath.

STOP
SPEE
LIMIT
25
WEIGHT
LIMIT
3
TONS
G.V.W.R.
NO
FISHING
ON
BRIDGE

"The Cure For A Heart Ache"

If only there was some medicine
I could take to relieve my pain.
And if only there was some simple way
To make you feel the same.

For a drum beats in my chest
A somber song it plays.
A sonnet filled with sorrow
Throughout these endless days.

All has lost its meaning
And nothing seems alright.
As if the light that was used for guiding
Made you lose your sight.

How can something inside me
Cause me so much pain?
For outside I show sunshine
When it's really pouring rain.

There has to be some simple way
To avoid this from the start.
For the only cure for a heart ache
Is to simply lose your heart.

"Kiss From A Rose"

Do you know of the feeling
When there are flowers all around?
When it's beauty is so astounding
And it's all just so profound.

Can you speak of the image
Of a daisy glowing bright?
With it's pedals so radiant
That everything seems right.

Could you describe the essence of a lily
And tell me why it sways?
It's glamour blowing in our hearts
Until the end of days.

Would you pluck the pedals of a tulip
To find your one true love?
When everything you could ever need
Comes from up above.

But I can't describe one flower
For it rises above the rest.
It's like a beacon of light in darkness
That no one could ever protest.

For how could anyone ever speak of your beauty?
For your radiance always flows.
That's why it would take all of eternity
To describe a kiss from a rose.

"The Death Of A Heart"

It knew not the perils of life.
The harsh reality that comes in view
And tares apart the heart in two.

Those words that make you lose control.
An earthquake of the dying soul.
That pushes you until you fall.

I can not express these words enough.
Or make a blind man see the truth.
And so I say without the proof.

My heart is dead,
Forever gone.
I bury it now.
Forever on.

"The World Within Her Eyes"

The light gleams through.
With one look into heavens gates
My soul takes flight.
Without any knowledge of wrong or right.

A breath I wish to take.
Her hand I wish to hold.
I see the beauty that lies within
A beauty lined with gold.

I wish to make her see this truth
I want to make her know.
But she will never hear my voice
My wound will only grow.

Now it all just seems too bleak
With much to my demise.
The only thing I wish to seek
Is that world within her eyes.

"If Only"

If only I could change the world
I know what I'd just do.
I'd match it to your beauty
So that all would know you're true.

If only I could take the stars from your eyes
I would fill the whole night's sky.
And use it to light the darkest paths
Until the day I die.

If only you could see yourself
The way that I see you.
I know that you'd then realize
That there could be no better view.

If only I could touch your heart
The way that you've touched mine.
I would make my way to heaven
Just to stop the hands of time.

If only I could find the words
To tell you how I feel.
I'd write a novel fit for kings
And leave nothing to conceal.

If only you knew how much I loved you
That's all that I would need to know.
But I fear that I will be left here waiting
With nothing left to show.

"The Forever Friend"

You see I've got this heart
That I keep trying to give
But people keep on breaking it
Just to see if I could live.

I keep hearing I'm amazing
And that I'm an outstanding guy.
But it seems it always ends up
With them saying good-bye.

I swear I get to the point
Where I feel I'm about to break.
Because what is a guy supposed to do
With a heart that no one will take?

I wish I could just find the girl
To take it off my hands.
Yet no matter who I seem to find
That famous statement stands.

I think you're great
But this has to end.
But how about
You just be my friend?

"If I Could Make You Love Me"

If I could make you love me
I would do what it takes.
I'd ravage this world
Until the ground shakes.

I would go to the cities
And rip down its walls.
Climb all the mountains
Just to watch as it falls.

I would give you the heavens
And all of the earth.
I would go down through hell
Just to show you my worth.

I'd gather the stars
And the sun's golden shine.
And give them to you
If then you'd be mine.

If I could make you love me
There is nothing I wouldn't do.
I would give all there is to give
If it meant you'd love me too.

"What I Want"

A girl that knows how to laugh.
Someone who can make me smile.
That would love to spend time together
Even for a little while.

A girl that appreciates
All the little things in life.
That's always dreamed of having a house
And becoming someone's wife.

A girl with eyes
That take my breath away.
As if I was gazing into a sunset
At the end of a beautiful day.

A girl who wants everything
But doesn't know what she wants at all.
That's always looking at the sky
Waiting for a star to fall.

A girl that wants a guy
That's as perfect as can be.
But is still incredibly happy
When all she gets is me.

"What She Wants"

A perfect man
With some perfect teeth.
And a perfect package
Right underneath.

A perfect gentleman
To escort her all around.
That knows when to speak
And not make a sound.

Some perfect eyes
That could see only her.
That shine right through darkness
Is what she would prefer.

A perfect body
Chiseled only to perfection.
That would match her perfect beauty
To make a true connection.

You see I'm really not that perfect
But for her I'm willing to try.
For she's captured my heart so perfectly
That without her I know I'd die.

"The Moment"

There was a time when I was happy.
When misery had no face.
And the radiance that surrounds me
Could be seen from any place.

No thing could make me falter.
No obstacles in my way.
No things that I would alter.
No wind could make me sway.

I was a king among men
And a man among a queen.
It was a moment none could touch
Or ever come between.

Yet time will always pass
As the moments come and go.
But no matter what will happen
There is one thing I will always know.

It's the moment time stood still
And everything was true.
What no other could ever fill.
The moment I had with you.

"Shattered Dreams"

I woke up to reality
With tears in my eyes.
No more happy days
No more golden skies.

Just a memory
Of a time once past.
Like the viewing of a sunset
It's gone all too fast.

If only I could wake
To a life with you there.
I would climb the highest mountain
To show you that I care.

For you seem to be the vision
That lies within my heart.
Yet whenever I awaken
It tares me all apart.

I know being awake
Isn't as wonderful as it seems
But it's better than being left
With all these shattered dreams.

"Because Of You"

Why do I always wish
Upon these distant stars?
As if something so far away
Could heal my depend scars.

Why do I pray
On these shattered knees each night?
As if someone were actually listening
And knew my every plight.

Why don't I stop
When I know I can't go on?
It's as if my heart won't stop beating
Even though it's already gone.

Why can't I move
Even though my legs work fine?
It's as if you went to heaven
And stole the sands of time.

To answer these questions
Is what I needed to do.
But I no longer need to search
For I found them all in you.

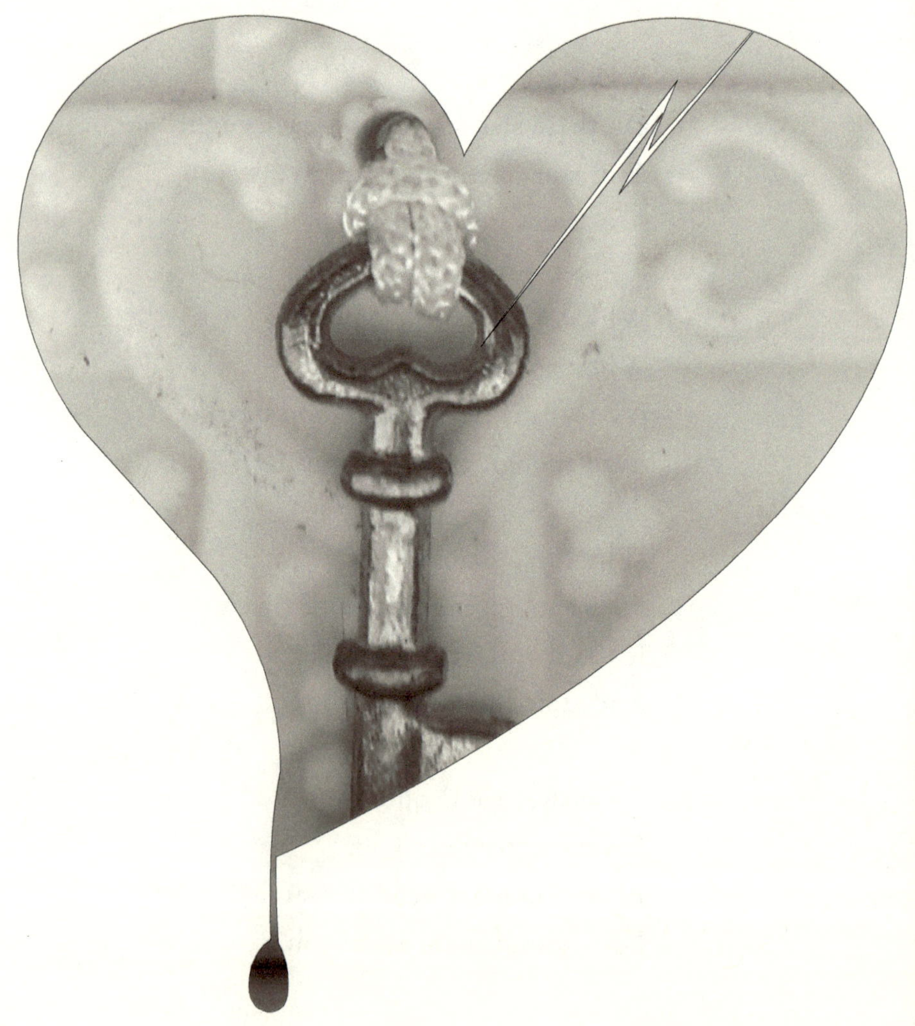

"The Key To Her Heart"

Deep in the brush
Past the towering trees
The place where no one looks
Is the place that no one sees.

Yet even in it's darkness
The light still shines through.
It shines its way into your eyes
It makes it all seem true.

Whose to say it isn't true?
What makes this place not real?
Does it mean you have to touch
In order just to feel?

I try to enter through
This place that sets me free.
But no matter where I look
I still can't find the key.

For now I'll sit at your door
One day you'll let me in.
My patience is eternal
But my hope is what wears thin.

"The Symphony Of The Night"

When the sun goes down
And the shadows come to play.
When the angles go to rest
And the demons come to stay.

When sanity makes no sense
And reality is unreal.
When life isn't lived
And when feelings have no feel.

When silence makes a sound
And the imagination takes control.
When words have no meaning
Yet you seem to know it all.

It's a refuge for the mind.
It's a vision with no sight.
It's a sanctum for the soul.
It's the symphony of the night.

"Far Cry"

Beauty in its prime.
Warmth from the sun's golden ray.
The meaning of existence.
The glory of each day.

She is the color to each flower.
With the radiance to match.
She is the silver in the lining
And the greatest in the batch.

She is the beat in my heart
And the heart to my soul.
She is the pinnacle of perfection
And the filling in each hole.

She is a dream in this reality
And I can't believe she's true.
She is the sunrise and the sunset
And the richness in the hue.

She is the words that I have written
For I would write them in the sky.
In hopes that she would wipe away
The tears from this far cry.

"Watching An Angel Walk Away"

In moments of sadness
And feelings of despair.
One looks for the answers
That are never really there.

Yet she came to me
Not in a vision or a dream.
But in the body of an angel
Within a heavenly beam.

She looked at me softly
With eyes that could heal the weak.
And walked right up towards me
With her angelic like physique.

She continued to walk
As if I wasn't there.
And then slowly began to vanish
Within the tranquil air.

She was everything that was in my heart
And I just wanted her to stay.
She was everything I ever wanted from this life
And I just watched her walk away.

"My Biggest Flaw"

Some people say I'm way too short
And others say I'm too tall.
Some people try to keep me up
While others just wait for the fall.

Some people say I'm not that smart
And the others will just agree.
Some people say that I should change
But they all don't really know me.

Some people think I'm ugly.
While the rest all think I'm fine.
Some people think I'm way too dark
While others agree that I shine.

Some people think I'm pushy
While others say that I'm shy.
Some people say I'm shady
But I think I'm a trustworthy guy.

Some people like to pick out your flaws
Right from the very start.
But some people just don't seem to know
That the biggest flaw is my heart.

"Why I Can Fly"

So I fell in love with her
It's not something I meant to do.
She just stepped right back into my life
And my feelings for her grew.

I know I've always known her
But it's different this time around.
See now this time were older
And things seem more profound.

It's just that feeling that I get
Whenever I hear her name.
It's like heaven is at my footstep
And that nothing will be the same.

But at the same time
I've never felt more afraid.
I fear that I am not enough for her
And soon in her eyes I will fade.

I just wish I had the courage
To tell her how I feel.
To expel all my fears inside
And to show her that I am real.

But alas here I stand
Waiting for a miracle to appear.
And pray that she will understand
Why I can fly when she is near.

"You And Me"

Take a moment if you will
To compare two souls.
Each with equal attributes
But both with different goals.

One's just a girl
That's always been so pretty.
With stars so bright inside of her eyes
It could light the darkest city.

And one just a boy
That's always looked to the skies.
Searching for the stars at night
That have fallen in her eyes.

She's been the girl
That all the guys have always wanted.
And he's been the boy
That all the people always taunted.

She's all he's wanted
Yet he could never break his chains.
For no mater how hard he tries
Still one thing remains.

She's just the girl
That gets all the glances.
And he's just a boy
Without many chances.

"Alone"

No matter how near
It is still too far.
No matter how bright
It is still too dark.

I wish this pain away
Each and every day.
I pray
Just to live a different way.

I stare at the stars
I hope to find my answers there.
Eternally I stare
Yet no longer do I care.

I still have hope.
I do not know why.
How can one have hope
If this world is a lie?

My journey is dark
I know this to be true.
But I will keep going
For it leads me to you.

"Broken Hearts and Distant Dreams"

Once again
He falls in love
And thinks this girl
Comes from above.

Yet watch in wonder
As the story unfolds
And see the boy
Give the heart that he holds.

For all that he wants
Is the love of his life.
To find the girl
He can then call his wife.

Yet as she grabs hold
Of the heart that he gives
She rips it apart
Just to see if he lives.

And now that boy
Truly knows what love means.
Nothing but broken hearts
And distant dreams.

"Dear God: The Last Letter"

Dear God,
This is my last letter.
I sent two before
Yet nothing got better.

People told me to ask you.
That you would make things right.
So I prayed during the day
And even at night.

They said to have patience.
To just hold my ground.
Yet whenever I looked
You could not be found.

I tried for so long.
I really tried hard.
But living this life
Has just left me scarred.

So instead of a letter
That just sits on a shelf
I'll end it today
And ask you myself.

"My Last Poem"

This is the last poem
That I write about your eyes.
Because it seems you've looked the other way
And left me to my demise.

This is the last poem
About how beautiful you really are.
Because you've left me with an open wound
That has turned into deepened scar.

This is the last poem
That will show how much I cared.
I will forget about any time we've spent
Any moments we've ever shared.

This is the last poem
That I write about my heart.
For I was only dreaming
I never had one from the start.

This is the last poem
That I'll ever write until death.
Maybe one day I'll change my mind
But I wouldn't be holding my breath.

"The End"

I cried today.
I shed the tears of a dying soul
Whose destiny could never be whole.
A life I could once, I can not control.

I tried today.
I tried to move on and live my life
To walk away and feel no strife.
But everywhere I look I can feel the knife
Deep in my heart taking my life.

I fell today.
I fell in love with a woman named fate.
She loved me once, but now will just hate.
She looks at me softly, but her eyes they now lie.
Telling me a story that I can't deny.

I ran today.
I ran away from the pain that's all around
And forever I will run until some hope is found.
But the road grows narrow and harder to run
And if I stop running my story is done.

It ends today
And always it will stop.
Staring at the edge
Waiting to drop.

www.ingramcontent.com/pod-product-compliance
Lightning Source LLC
LaVergne TN
LVHW091633100826
845152LV00001B/17

9780615208732